Brain Trots & Heart Garbage

Poems I

by

Gary R. Gowers

Brain Trots & Heart Garbage - Poems I © 2024 Gary R Gowers. Names, characters, places, and incidents either are the product of the author's imagination or are used with expressed written permission.

This work, including all characters, names, and places: Copyright 2024 Gary R Gowers, unless otherwise noted.
Cover art provided by Gary R Gowers.
Layout by Edward Gehlert.

No part of this book may be reproduced or transmitted in any form or by any means, electronic or mechanical, including photocopying, recording, or by any information storage and retrieval system, without the written permission of both the publisher and author.

All rights reserved.

Happy Duck Publishing
P.O. Box 607
Belle, MO 65013
Genre: Poetry
ISBN: 978-1-7369596-7-1

This collection is dedicated to

<u>Debra Marie McCoy</u>

aka my Ma

Acknowledgments

I'd like to thank Mark McClane and Tony Hayden of the Osage Arts Community (OAC) for their continued support in the development of projects such as this, as well as for providing a roof over my head and food in my belly. The work they do in providing the time and space to explore creative avenues is invaluable.

In regards to being a source of encouragement and confidence, Edward and Eva Gehlert have been supreme. I thank them from the bottom of my heart for having the energy to read every sentence that shows up in their inboxes, and for taking those files and putting them into book form.

Lastly, it is necessary to acknowledge all of the people that have inspired me to write about them, in both a positive and negative light. Without them, this goofy shit wouldn't exist. In some cases, it would have been better if it didn't.

TABLE OF CONTENTS

9. Brain Trots & Heart Garbage
10. Neverending, 'Til It Does
13. And the Theys Say It
14. Everyone Has an Ilsa
15. 3:51 AM
17. Listen to the Frogs
18. Belly Up
21. Kai Tak
22. Hack
24. Lies and Truth
25. Easy Peasy
28. Peristalsis
31. Dumb and Dangerous
32. Always Welcome
33. Two Men
35. Zap
37. A Great Start
39. "..." people
42. The Two-Headed Man
44. In the Next Life (Or the One After That)
47. Boo Hoo du Jour
50. Wet Pages
52. Misdemeanor
53. Fizzle
54. Mystery of the Ages
59. 95%
61. Different Ways of Being the Same
63. No Thanks
64. Specimens
66. Anatomy
67. Travel in Style

71. BIG DAY!
75. A Tweaker Pays by Debit
77. Doomed Love Affair
78. The Past
79. Mixed Blessing
81. Log on the Red Oak
84. Pop In
86. Eyelash Perm
88. Tug of War Infinitum
89. Public Transit
91. The Best By Far
93. Do the Work
94. Unrealized
95. Big If
96. A Real Drag
98. Texas Oasis
103. Warm Beer
105. Morning Dew
107. Crunch Crunch Crunch
109. The Prize
110. Night Pains
112. Zillions
115. Sawed Off Bastards
118. Safe Assumption
120. Golden Noodles
122. Red Flag
126. Good Riddance
128. Fucked Proper
130. If It Had Been So
132. Advice from a Jailhouse Regular
133. Picky
135. To the Death
136. The Man Who Works for Dogs

138. The Price of Experience
139. Hip Shot
141. J. D. & Me
143. G. R. G. & I
145. fool no longer
147. Holidays
148. Mantis Boy
150. Fine Young Cannibal
152. Advice to Young Girls
154. The Day Phleebit Came to Town
156. Being Human is Tragic Enough Without the Window Dressing
159. Rarities
160. Beautiful Death
161. Burning Innovators
163. Requiem for a Varmint
165. All is Well at Rock Bottom
167. Stay in Bed
172. Fist Fight
174. Big Gals and Skinny Dudes
177. Casualty
178. A Royal Death
180. Kick a Man When He's Down
182. Any Given Night in Seoul ROK
185. The Authority
188. The Giant
190. 600
194. Eggs and Toast
197. Yellow Fever
200. Loins
202. Chemical Warfare
204. Trade In
209. Lowest of the Low

210. Goofy Food Shit
213. The Stardust High Horse
215. Speaking of the Dead
217. A Lesson Hardly Learned

Brain Trots and Heart Garbage

My brain must have gotten a hold of some

Tandoori Chicken

left on the counter overnight

because it has the trots and

is spilling shit out on my keyboard.

And what isn't diarrhea is just

plain old plebeian garbage,

refuse left over from past

relationships, disappointments and failures.

Neverending, 'Til It Does

Beep Beep Beep

The starting pistol to begin yet another

day of routine servitude.

Roll out grunting and put on the coffee and

smoke, if you do, waiting on the brew.

Caffeine and Nicotine, friends in need,

raise the eyelid sails so you can see

what's on the horizon.

Not that you need to see 'cause you've

done it thousands of times before.

You know exactly what's out there, for the most part.

Breathing beating circulating defecating urinating

slumbering seeing hearing smelling eating tasting.

Fine and

dandy,

no real effort expended, second nature.

All nature, rather.

It's the showering scrubbing brushing applying flushing pouring cooking washing organizing dressing tying tucking going.

The work around the working,

the choring, the maintaining

and keeping things moving, the keeping up.

Keeping up with things that, ironically,

don't matter for shit anyway.

Tasks! Maintenance! Chores!

Numberless units of doing.

Often doing for someone else.

The building blocks of the slow death.

Being dead would be easy, it's the dying that takes effort.

Living is so tedious some days, it doesn't seem worth it.

Scratch that. No "seem" about it. Not worth it at all.

Not a lick. But do it anyway.

If it looks like a duck and sounds like a duck.

Beep Beep Beep

Here we go again.

And the Theys Say It

Everything you write is doom and gloom

They say.

You should write something cheerful and upbeat

They say.

Try looking on the bright side of life

They say.

Let a smile be your umbrella

They say.

They say

They say

They say a lot and maybe

They have a point but

They

Ain't

Me.

Everyone Has an Ilsa

I enjoyed the flick as a kid,

though I was unimpressed with Rick's crybaby attitude,

that dim night in the Café Américain,

as Sam's fingers tickled the ivories.

Rick had it all.

He was handsome, cynical and worldly,

and had the coolest saloon

in French Morocco.

Why was he carrying on like that?

It was only much later,

when I was left standing in my own rain shower,

hurt, confused and enraged,

that I understood why he hid himself away and

simmered.

3:51 AM

3:51 am is a magical time

when improbabilities look like possibilities

the conscious is working like

a Rubik's Cube

matching up colors on each side

making sense of daylight confusions

inevitabilities are more acceptable

and a little less frightening

knowing that's how it's got to be

because that's how it's always been

and there is nothing special enough

about you

to enable a rerouting of the time stream

the well-intentioned half truths you hear

from those who mean well

but lack the conviction

to carry out their high-minded words

seem less deliberate

and more of a flaw in human nature

failing at high-minded pronouncements

is much more forgivable

than succeeding at low-minded schemes

one more cigarette

and then it's time to put away the cube

until tomorrow's darkness

and sleep the sleep of the kind-hearted fool

Listen to the Frogs

It took me decades of work;

Listening,

    Recording,

Transcribing,

    Translating

And listening some more.

Summer after summer, night after night

Down at the pond, dusk till dawn.

It was a mission, important only to me,

To learn what the frogs were saying.

I poured my life into the pursuit,

Only to learn they were talking about me,

And all the time and effort I was wasting.

Belly Up

The rural equivalent

of Arthur's

round table.

The bed of a

pick-up truck.

Ford, Chevy, Dodge, GMC

even Toyota,

debatably.

Big-bellied men

who work, grind, toil at

farming, constructing, welding,

mechanicing, trucking, laboring,

or what have you.

Important men, necessary men,

the backbone

of a nation.

Belly up to the bed,

coolers full of beer,

jerky and chips and candy bars,

to carry on about carrying on.

They can tell you how to fix any

problem that comes to mind.

They know what to do about

the illegal immigrants

the needy minorities

the perverted homosexuals

the mouthy women

the disrespectful children

the mayhem of mass media

the lies in social media

the illusions of politics.

You name it,

they can fix it.

You want to know about

religion or UFOs,

catfish bait or deer scent,

Bigfoot or Big Pharma,

engines or plumbing,

JFK or 9/11,

depression or drag shows.

They know about everything.

They'll fill you in.

Yet they can't

make it home

without a

DUI.

Kai Tak

Table stowed and seat in the upright position.

Coming in low, or so it seems.

Only because the tenements are high.

Weaving a path through homes

Close enough to see red days on calendars

And to count the buttons on shirts hung to dry.

Close enough to look children in the eyes

From your window seat in the cattle car.

Touch down, tires squalling, rubber smoke rising

On a lick of tarmac junting into the sea

Firmly on the ground and all is well.

Kowloon doesn't register the fears or reliefs

Of one more round-eyed *gweilo.*

*gweilo: Cantonese for *foreigner*

Hack

Check
    It
        Out!
I'm
    Not
        Writing
            In
                Regular
                    Line
                        Form!
                    The
              Mark
          Of
        A
      Poetry
    Hack.

I

  Should

    Probably

      Use

        A

          Word

            Like

          Void

        Or

      Abyss

    For

Dramatic effect!!!

Somebody just shoot me already.

Put me out of your misery.

Lies and Truth

A lie told through tears

is still a lie.

A truth told by an asshole

is still a truth.

The source of the reality

is not relevant.

But it greatly influences

what is believed.

And so here

we are.

The truth treated

as lies.

Lies treated

as the truth.

Easy Peasy

Writing is easy.

All you have to do is take a really sharp blade,

a freshly sharpened straight razor is best,

or maybe a scalpel,

and run it up your wrists in line with the main veins,

not across like in the movies.

Or you can slice it across your throat,

ear to ear, but you gotta cut deep.

The big femoral arteries in your inner thighs

are good, too.

Once you've opened yourself up, wherever,

you just let everything pour out across the paper or

the monitor, whichever medium you're using.

If you're really wanting to punch it to the reader,

take that blade and, starting at your belly button,

slice up towards your throat and let your intestines,

lungs, spleen, heart and the rest just spill in a heap.

If you like a cerebral flair in your prose, you gotta go for the head, but that takes a ball peen hammer or a chainsaw, so be willing to work for it.

If you're a romance writer, it's much easier, you just squat and piss and/or shit it out right there.

No editing necessary. And that's okay.

If you're having trouble figuring out the best method for your work, I'll give you some examples that might help.

Fyodor Dostoevski cut the femoral artery in each leg and gushed across the paper.

Charles Bukowski slit his wrists and his throat, and then took a big dump in the puddle of blood.

E. L. James jacked off a dozen middle-aged men and flung the jizz at the monitor.

Umberto Eco smashed his skull in with a sledgehammer

and scrambled his brains about.

Everyone does it in their own way,

whatever is right for them.

And none of them are wrong.

Find yours.

Easy peasy.

Peristalsis

Your body is doing it right now.

Muscles in your intestines,

undulating in waves,

for the singular purpose of moving shit,

aka waste,

from your personal temple,

aka your body.

There is another waste removal process in progress,

as well,

in an invisible canal leading from the brain directly to

the mouth,

but unlike the completely involuntary muscle

movements that

purge you of shit,

the brain-mouth highway is controllable and trainable.

Diarrhea of the mouth is a curable condition.

In your ass you have a sphincter,

a starfish gateway,

that pinches off shit into disposable segments,

aka turds.

And you flush them away.

Sense and love and decency,

these are

sphincters of the brain,

of thought.

These can be used at will,

for good or evil,

your choice

to make.

You can flush the turds

or

let them float,

to disgust, sicken, annoy, offend

the next guy.

Dumb and Dangerous

The penis is mentally deficient

and, if it could talk,

it would stutter.

Feel no pity for the penis

and show it no trust,

for it will bite like a

wounded pet.

Always Welcome

Everyone has a place in this world.

If you are hot and slutty that place is anywhere you want it to be.

Two Men
for MCG

There are no words to describe

the difference between

what I am

and

what I should have been.

They are two different men

with the same face

only

one is smiling

and

one is pretending to smile.

They are both crazy, though,

just one would have been crazy

about you

and

the other is capital "C" insane.

Zap

Driving home in a storm last night

                        thunder booming lightning

flashing

Water cascading down my windshield

                        the wipers working to keep up

with the deluge

An ultra-bright bolt from Zeus struck

                        the blacktop directly in front of

my truck

The charge caused the hair on my arms

                        to vibrate in place and stand on

tippy-toes

My eyes were blinded for a long moment

                        the smell of the very air was

transformed

I remembered that sensation and it petrified me

that is what it feels like to fall in love.

A Great Start

Let me start this with a joke.

"What did the overweight girl with low

self-esteem say to the abusive alcoholic?"

The answer?

"I do."

He was an alcoholic when they dated,

he was an alcoholic when he knocked her up,

he was an alcoholic when he proposed.

She was stone sober when she accepted.

And she wondered why people weren't

jumping for joy.

Her dad warned her, her brothers warned her but

"they didn't know what they were talking about".

She could change him.

He just needed love and patience and understanding.

The night of the wedding he and his friends got

drunk and started shit with a wedding guest.

A great start.

But she'd change him.

Of course, she would.

"..." people

Here is a modern

Social media tech phenom

For you.

There are people out there

With only PART of something to say,

I call them the "... people".

Say you make a post

Instagram Facebook TikTok what-have-you

And the post inspires a response of some sort.

But the person posting the comment

Only gives you a part of their response

And then a "...", that's right a "...".

For example, I make a post:

"I don't care for dogs, I think they are overrated."

The response: "Well, dogs are man's best friend…"

…

…

…

Yeah? And?

What comes after the "…"?

Do you even know what comes after the "…"?

Am I supposed to tell you what comes after the "…"?

I've been thinking on it and I've concluded

The person is offended

but afraid to be too confrontational.

Or the person is trying to sound smart

but runs out of smarts and can't finish.

Or the person never had a point to begin with but wanted to chime in hoping they'd think of something along the way.

Or the person is hoping to draw me in with the mysterious "…"
in order to facilitate a conversation or argument over the comment.

Or maybe they're just plain lazy or noncommittal.

I don't know…

I just wish…

And then they can…

…

…

The Two-Headed Man
for Rosie Grier

Back in '72

Rosey Grier and Ray Milland

Were in a movie called

The Thing With Two Heads.

Milland's head was transplanted

Onto Grier's body

Right next to Rosey's head.

There they were, cheek to cheek.

Grier's character

Was a black convict

Milland's character

Was a racist surgeon.

Milland came up with the surgery

'Cause he was dying and needed a body.

I think it was a weird mix of sci-fi,

Racism examination and O. Henry.

It's going to take me

Many nights wondering

Lots of coffee and Luckies

To figure out why there wasn't a sequel.

In the Next Life (Or the One After That)
for MCG

It's all a fantasy, of course,

but in the next life

we'll be back.

The users and betrayers and addicts and creepers,

they'll be slugs and worms and centipedes and gnats.

But we'll be back,

as we could have, should have been.

It's far-fetched, I know,

but in the next life

we'll be back.

The feedings and burping and bathings and rocking to sleep,

the first day of school and the recitals and the plays and the homework.

We'll be back for that,

as we should have, might have been.

It's a long-shot, to be sure,

but in the next life

we'll be back.

The loving and the hugging and the kissing on the cheek

and the tucking into bed,

and also the fighting and the yelling and the rebelling

and the giving of the

stink eye.

We'll be back for all of that,

as we might have, ought to have been.

It's not guaranteed, it's a fact,

but in the next life

we'll be back.

They'll come knocking at the door due to your beauty

your grace your kindness,

but very few will be worthy and you'll know which is which - I'll make sure of that.

We'll be back for these things,

as we ought to have, would have been.

It's the thinnest of hopes, to be honest,

but in the next life

we'll be back.

I'll grow old like I'm doing now but not by myself as I'm doing now,

I'll have a little one or two to spoil as I did you, maybe spoil even more.

We'll be back for what we didn't have this time around,

as we should have been.

Here is a rhyme, just for you,

to bring this little musing to an end.

"Maybe in the next life, if that idea holds any water,

I'll be your father and you'll be my daughter."

Boo Hoo du Jour

You say somebody stepped on your feelings today?

Oh, that's too bad.

A little kid just died from intestinal parasites in

Ecuador, but

being called sir when your Biceps are bigger than mine

and your

Voice is as deep as Sam Elliott's, and with the very same

Mustache.

How dare they not know you feel like Jenna Ortega

today?

That is so very much worse.

A lady pushing her baby in a stroller on her way to the

grocery was triggered three times,

the baby only once,

but it doesn't take much hot lead

To take out a baby.

I'm just glad you found a safe space to recover from

somebody eating a Snickers, throwing all caution,

in regards to your peanut allergy, to the wind.

Selfish bastard.

Eating something he likes and not

knowing your medical history.

Yeah, sure, there is an island of garbage the size of

Texas

floating around in the Pacific Ocean.

But, okay, I'll focus on the fact that gas went up a dime

and it'll cost you more to run around buying fountain

drinks

with your porker wife and four mangy kids, one being

yours,

maybe,

in your side-by-side.

Oui c'est vrai, we all feel pain

but some pains are worse

than others so

get your finger out of your ass

and switch on perspective.

And if you can't see that, I don't care,

your idiocy is my pain

to bear.

Everyone is equal and the same,

but only your pain is special.

Funny how that works.

Wet Pages

The weather app said sunny and clear.

I should have known better than to trust

anything from this century

tech-wise.

But I finished my last read last night.

And the thought of not having a story

to dive into tonight was giving

me the erps.

I should have taken the bag as offered.

But they are made of plastic and

seem to always end up murdering

the turtles.

But the summer rain has the worms and frogs out.

The worms cause they will drown down under

and the frogs are going feed frenzy on the worms

so abundant.

The worms are not watching where they are going.

The frogs are too focused on the worms

and I am trying to keep my books dry so, sorry,

squish squish.

I blame the weather app for this manslaughter.

Wormslaughter and frogslaughter, rather,

and so they are collateral damage of my mission

to read.

Misdemeanor

I got pulled over by a state trooper last night.

He not only ticketed me for not rhyming my words,

He also revoked my poetic license.

Fizzle

Start with a BANG, end with a BANG.

There is plenty of time in the middle to fizzle.

Mystery of the Ages

An old

paper towel

blotted with,

I don't know,

is that

coffee?

tea?

Blood?

Why did you

fold it up

and

put it

in the book?

and leave

it there

for years?

Was it a

keepsake of

some kind,

for some

occasion

or

other?

Why was

this dirty

disposable

paper towel

important enough

to preserve

in the pages of

a book?

That doesn't

seem like

you.

Were you

somewhere

that lacked

the proper

trash

receptacle

and you kept

it to throw away

later

but forgot?

You loved

books.

You wouldn't

treat a

book

that way without

a reason.

What was

it?

Did it

remind you

of

someone

something

someplace

or all

three?

You're gone

now

and I can't

ask you

the significance.

The meaning.

The reason.

If any.

All that's left

is to

Thank You

for this

Mystery

of

the

Ages.

95%

It was in

the early 90s.

I was at an

airport, a big one.

Chicago or Los Angeles,

maybe Dallas.

An older man,

black and dressed nice.

He rushed by but

caught my eye.

I'm 95% sure it was

Nipsey Russell.

Different Ways of Being the Same

You begrudge anything new that you don't understand

While you shuffle from your bed to the toilet to your

bed to the toilet.

You do cartwheels and hit the clubs with your painted

posse

But in the back of your mind you're worried about the

rent and the next car payment.

Your legs won't hold you long enough to stand in a

ticket line

Though you've been waiting with giddy glee for this

sequel to be released.

You know she would dig you if she got to know your

mindworks

But all she can see is the cane holding you up and the stoop in your posture.

Endless descriptions of people with wrinkled and unwrinkled faces

And they are all Old.

No Thanks

When I was a kid

I saw two dogs locked in copulation

ass to ass

standing in a yard for everyone to see.

School chums whispered pre-pubescent

theories about S. E. X.

I said it looked embarrassing and boring

No, thank you.

Specimens

Somehow they escape the petri dishes

and slip slide squirm

out into the world.

You see them them taking up space

in convenience stores and Walmarts

and fast food "restaurants".

You'll know them by their

bad ink bad dye jobs vape pens

asses hanging out of shorts and shit band T-shirts.

You'll hear them

giggling belching cussing farting

as they peruse the

candy aisles and fountain drink stations.

You'll smell them coming before you see them,

melon menthol Monster energy Axe body wash

patchouli pot Fireball.

Their progeny mimicking

the noises the smells the looks

whining for

sugar caffeine plastic junk.

My socialist leanings take a beating every time they

waddle into my world.

Anatomy

I've a

poem in my heart

a song on my tongue

an apple in my eye

kind words on my lips

music in my ears

a spring in my step

feelings in my gut

time on my hands

love on my mind

But I'm mostly worried

about the blood in my

Urine.

Travel in Style

I had been eating Korean food, kimchi rice and such,

for a full year in Seoul

before I headed for Rome and destinations beyond.

It came time for the in-flight meal and I chose

something with cheese

and that was all she wrote,

the high fat high carb greasy food attacked without

mercy.

The diarrhea hit fast and hard and had me in the coffin-

sized

bathroom for half the trip,

and while ass-purging I noticed my dick was dripping

through my pants.

The dick drip intensified and burned when I pissed gonorrhea-style,

and after bouts of the squirts

I was using half a roll to wipe and another half to wrap my pecker.

It was a terrible way to travel, guts exploding and penis slobbering away like that,

a lobotomized resident of an experimental sanitarium.

I touched down in Rome and set out to see what's to see,

but spent most of my time

begging restaurants and shops to let me use their bathrooms.

I was shitting all over Rome and leaving a drip trail of

dick infection

in my wake, everywhere I went,

I was pinballing from bathroom to bathroom amongst

the Roman ruins.

I took a train through the Alps going to Paris but

couldn't shit while

stopped at stations 'cause

the liquid feces emptied out right on the tracks and

nobody likes that.

Once I made it to Paris I told my pal about my sick gut

and my sick manhood,

and so he took me to a clinic

where they shot me with penicillin and gave me

industrial-strength Pepto.

So my advice to you if you are ever inclined to travel abroad with loose bowels and loose morals, make sure it is somewhere with a socialized health care system.

BIG DAY!
for They Know Who They Are

Today's the big day!

A bed opened up and

you gotta go!

I'm so happy for us!

What am I talking about?

Why, the home we're putting you in,

of course!

Why?

You don't move fast enough

to suit us.

You can't formulate your thoughts

and express yourself fast enough

to suit us.

Oh, and let's not forget about how

we have to H-E-L-P you to the

bathroom.

That doesn't suit us one little bit!

So we're going to pack up your

entire life in a couple of bags

and move you right in!

Don't worry, you'll have pictures

of us on your side of the room so

you can look up and see the faces

of the people you brought into the world,

but who then turned around and

abandoned you!

Because you didn't suit us!

You'll love it!

You get to keep snacks in

your room!

And you can have a mini-fridge!

You're gonna have a nice

stranger for a roommate and

nice strangers to take care of you!

You're gonna love it!

Don't worry, we'll pop in

and remind you of how

great you have it!

You don't want to go?

Well, of course, you don't,

but that doesn't matter, not

even a little bit!

You've become a hindrance

you see, a burden.

We have things to do,

lives to live, families to raise.

Absolutely, you're family, too.

But you get in the way,

you're not as important

as the rest of us.

Surely, you can understand that.

What if it was me?

Don't be silly!

MY kids would never

do this to me.

You need to use the bathroom?

We'll let a nurse take care

of that when we get

you there.

Away from here,

away from the people

you were silly enough

to trust.

But don't forget:

We love you, mom!

A Tweaker Pays By Debit

Hi there, Twitchy.

Will this be all for you today?

Insert your card whenever you're ready.

Wait...

You took it out too soon.

Put it back in, please.

Let me...

No, put it in again.

Give it a sec for the transaction.

No, it wasn't done.

Put it in again.

It's not...

It wasn't finished.

Put it back.

Now your PIN number.

Put it back.

PIN number.

It is saying the PIN is wrong.

Put it back.

Try your PIN again.

No…

Put it back.

And the PIN.

Let me enter…

Put it back.

Don't touch it.

PIN.

Don't touch it.

Leave it.

Wait.

It says "Insufficient Funds".

Yes, you can pay by cash.

Doomed Love Affair

There's no telling how far it'll go;

'cause that's just how life is - unknowable.

Unexpected but expected in an odd twisted way.

Two magnets in a junk heap

somehow make their way into an embrace,

shocked at the likelihood, the very chance

of unintended, but welcome, union.

A rollercoaster with no seat belts,

gravity the saving grace,

dips and loops and whirligigs of up and down

perpetually scared shitlessness.

Pop goes the weasel, kerplunk goes the anvil;

like the wily coyote on the endless chase,

after a bird with no meat on its bones, but too much

invested to stop now.

The Past

Just the whisperings

of a ghost.

Whistle a different tune

and it fades to nothing.

For nothing it is

and nothing it was.

A recollection more than

a memory.

Soon forgotten, of course,

since it never existed.

Mixed Blessing

A homeless man sits

on a hot concrete curb

holding a sign:

ANYTHING HELPS

A rotund woman in

a floral print dress

spots him and clops over

in over-strained heels.

The homeless man looks

up at her, hopefully, as

the woman digs a hand

into her bra,

just over her heart,

and pulls out a $20,

folded over several times over

and soaked through

with titty sweat.

She hands the sodden

bill to the homeless man

and then walks proudly

away having done her part.

The homeless man continues

to sit on the concrete curb

holding the folded bill by a

corner with the tips of two wet fingers,

staring and grinning at his

mixed blessing.

Log on the Red Oak

There's a big log

out there in the woods,

just up the bank

from Red Oak Creek.

It's high enough up

to avoid the spring swell

and the overgrowth

hides it from plain view.

I'm going to hollow out

that log, it's big enough

to sit up in, and smooth

out the interior and make

the floor flat and even.

I'm going to carve shelves

into the walls on the inside

and run a stove pipe through

the side at the furthest end.

I'll line my books up on the

shelves, maybe drill holes to

hold pens and pencils,

put in a little camp stove to

cook and provide a little warmth,

and finally lay down a bed of

quilts my grandmother made and

rest my head on a red cushion with

tassels at the corners.

I'll eat rabbits I catch in snares,

fish from the creek, berries from

the bushes and mushrooms growing

on my log, I'll fetch water from the

Red Oak in a bucket for brewing

my coffee and washing my face.

Once I have everything ready,

the big log now a home, I'll phase

myself out of this 21st century circus

of greed and lust and violence and circuits.

To hell with it, I've created heaven.

Sorry, no forwarding address.

Pop In

Sleep-heavy eyes snap open

at the sound of its steps coming down the walk

popping in

just to bare its fangs and reopen scars.

Tip-toes up to the door to

rap one knuckle ever-so-lightly to say that it is

popping in

under the door like a rancid mist.

Never bother to hide from it

for it goes room to room until it finds you

popping in

you inhale the crazy in your non-hiding spot.

No rhyme or reason as to

why it chose today to come around

popping in

letting you know it still exists and hasn't died.

It's angrier than usual

because it is finding it harder to find you

popping in

to do damage and leave only by force of your will.

Eyelash Perm

The mirror

shows me

I have

work

to do.

where did all the muscle tone go, skin just hanging

around like truant children,

from the neck the arms under the eyes, eyes that need

to squint to make out the

disappointment staring back at me, do some sit ups

some push ups some pull ups

tone that shit up only takes some repetition, stand a

little taller with posture in mind

why stoop when you can stand ramrod straight, fool the

gravity with arrogance instead

sagging tits sagging belly sagging ass, tattoos look like

they're melting over themselves

nose is a bit bigger than yesterday ears are bigger than

ever, teeth going yellow like

the whites of my eyes, hairs are where they shouldn't be

growing around growths

Lots of

work

to do

I'll start

with

perming my

eyelashes.

Tug of War Infinitum

Alive is alive,

dead is dead.

The middle doesn't matter,

except it does.

Or not.

Public Transit

It was weird enough meeting

an octopus on the bus.

But to make it weirder, this was

the most positive thinking fellow

you could imagine.

One of the optimistic octopi,

that's what he was alright.

Sitting at the end of the row in a

burnt orange jumpsuit and four pair

of Air Jordans.

I asked him,

"What do you think of global homogeneity?"

He didn't skip a beat,

"I think it's damned fine, maybe we'll all get along,"

he said.

"But aren't you concerned about diminishing cultural expression?" I asked.

"Not in the least," he said, "The cream will rise to the top."

The bus stopped at my corner and I got off, my stomach growling. I was in the mood for seafood but I went to a chicken joint out of respect for optimism.

The Best By Far

Drugs, soft and hard,

mostly soft but in great quantities.

Lithe darlings, shimmy and coo,

wanting only to please in that moment.

Fat paydays, with little effort,

the coffers full to play with at will.

Far-off destinations, spicy and exotic,

full of sights, sounds, smells and experiences.

All great, all number-one-grade-A-wonderful

but the best feeling by far

Is to wake up without an alarm,

roll your surprisingly still-breathing

carcass out of the sack,

put on a pot of coffee,

light up a Lucky,

and sit quiet and safe

in solitude and the realization

that you have nowhere to be

and the entire goddamned day is your own.

Do The Work

He longed to love

and to be loved

tit for tat

The head of the table

and to be called "father"

How was school today?

To be known

or at the least

to be respected in turn

and maybe remembered

A creator of snappy passages

new generations

and unrivaled experiences

He only pined

but never did

The silly sumbitch.

Unrealized
for MCG

The seed was planted

and it started to grow.

But the flower was trampled

before it could bloom.

Still,

the fragrance is sweet

and the colors are brilliant.

Even if only in my dreams.

Big If
for MCG

If Einstein was right

And parallel dimensions exist

Then maybe you are laughing now

Maybe we are laughing together

Up past bedtime but that's okay

Because there it is a Merry Christmas

And that makes this second in time

In this dimension sweet and good

And I can smile a little.

A Real Drag

Crackpots sit in dim rooms dreaming up schemes concerning love affairs, revolutions and economic health.

They are the true geniuses,

but the average John and Jane Doe are ignorant to this fact.

They are content to feed and breed,

making more little Does to populate an already-inhospitable

community of con-men, whores, sadists and spoiled children.

The pets rule the roost if we're being honest,

shedding and shitting on the creations of their masters because...

I'm not sure why.

Because they show gratitude or unconditional love or

loyalty?

And that gives them power.

That's the key to getting along right there; no power struggle;

no contention, no innovation, no thought-out premeditation,

just puppy dog eyes and a winning smile and you'll go a long

way in this world, baby.

It's all such a self-righteous, beautiful drag.

Texas Oasis

I never liked that song by

Oasis - *Champagne Supernova.*

I like the name, but that's about

it.

Roughly seven-and-a-half

minutes of Liam Gallagher

mewling and whining through his

nose.

Shitty song,

but

good name.

I was in my first year teaching

English in Asia, me

and

a bunch of Canadians.

They didn't like me much,

some kind of "little brother" syndrome

or some such

shit.

They thought Americans are

loud and cocky and domineering

and

they're right.

But when John Hock came along,

they started to appreciate my

mild-mannered Missourian ways,

for Hock was a

Texan

and all that entails.

He was big, not so tall, but wide,

and brash,

and freakishly strong,

and loud

and in-your-face friendly.

He played rugby

and

liked to horse around,

punch you in the shoulder to

punctuate a joke.

The Canadians hated him;

I found

him hilarious.

We clicked from the get-go,

he's a big guy, I'm a big guy,

we popped each others' backs,

nobody else could do it for us.

We both drank, in large amounts.

We were both educated rednecks

that liked to hear ourselves

talk.

I'll tell you something else

about that big ole Texan,

"Ham-Hock", as I called him,

that sumbitch could sing.

I was at his place

and

he was showering, we were about

to hit the town,

when I heard

Champagne Supernova

coming from his bathroom.

Just him, not singing to the radio.

Blew my mind.

So I like the name of the song,

and

I like how "Ham-Hock"

sang

It.

Warm Beer

You just keep on keeping on

even though you know

one of these days,

and you don't know which,

it'll be lights out.

I always felt bad about when my dad died,

on a Friday morning.

It's bad enough that he died,

but the man really enjoyed his free time.

After all those years of work work and more work,

he deserved a

last weekend.

If there is a God above, which is laughable,

he's/she's/it's/they're pretty much a

first-rate prick.

A benevolent God wouldn't let a man ice down beer for the weekend only to let it get warm.

Morning Dew
for Jason E. A. G.

Outside at the crack of dawn

ready to take on the day.

My brother was outside having

a smoke in the cool, spring air.

I walked up to where he was

leaning against the back of

the truck and noticed the beads

of dew speckling every surface.

I reached down and ran my

finger along the metal ball of

the trailer hitch, "Dewy," said I.

"I just peed on that," he answered.

That's a little life lesson for you;

before you go sticking your fingers

into things you should know the

difference between dew and piss.

Crunch Crunch Crunch

Late one night after a long drawn-out conversation

about

things mental

Me and the crazy girl decided to go out on the back

porch

for a smoke

The porch light was on and countless insects were

whirling

and dancing

around the porch light as insects are known to do

including

June bugs

Some of the June bugs lay stunned on the porch such

clumsy

inept flyers

The crazy girl looked down at them and started to

slowly step

on them

One by one just slowly put her weight down on the June

bugs

one at a time

Listen to how they crunch crunch crunch she said

grinning

Crazy-ass beetle-murdering bitch.

The Prize

I look at myself in the mirror now and wonder,

"How did I do it?"

My big bloated belly, my shrunken muscles,

my nearsighted eyes and the arthritis in my joints.

The odd growths on my skin, some cancerous, for sure.

My wheezing oxygen-starved lungs and my bad back.

"How did I do it?"

I'm not much to look at now,

but one time, decades ago,

half of me swam in a race against millions of half-others

and won!

Sitting here wondering how I did it in the first place is

the

Prize.

Night Pains

It's in the wee hours,

the still, quiet hours,

when lonely and alone feel much

the same.

The wounds that scar over

in day's light

shielding themselves from the glare

of the world

break open and resume their seeping.

Regret and grief and could-have-beens

stain the sheets

only to disappear temporarily

in the morning light.

At those times,

the living and the dead are

one and the same,

both out of sight, but

vivid in memory's eye.

Zillions

There are zillions of things you could be doing right now.

Wiping dust from the window sills

Shaving the dog

Standing on the shoulders of giants

Working on the cure for male pattern baldness

Hosting a Humphrey Bogart film festival

Picking those dark specks out of the butter

Daydreaming about the girl in the front row

Checking the air in your tires

Weeding your garden

Cleaning the angels off the heads of your pins

Double-checking the spelling in your report

Trimming your ear hair

Thinking about what a camel hump looks like on the inside

Turning down the thermostat

Reading the new Stephen King

Scrubbing at the stubborn ring in the tub

Following your wife to see if she's cheating

Planning that three-day weekend at the Gulf Shores

Changing the water filter

Singing in the shower

Planning nutritious meals for the kiddies

Tripping the light fantastic

Saving for a rainy day

Worrying about that weird growth on your shoulder

There are zillions of things you could be doing right now

But you're reading a list of options

Made by a guy who could be doing zillions of other things

Sawed Off Bastards

1

I came home late in a darkness rivaling squid ink.

When I shut the door to my truck I dropped my keys in the overgrown grass.

I searched and searched, mostly blind, but couldn't find the damned things.

After twenty minutes a little voice said, "Hey, buddy. Looking for these?"

A gnome, eight inches tall and wearing a red hat, was holding my keys.

"Thanks, man." I took my keys from his tiny hand and offered him a beer.

The next night I came home late, another night of squid ink darkness.

I got out of my truck with my hands full and tripped, sprawling out in the grass.

"Hey, buddy. You looking for this stuff?"

Two gnomes in red hats were holding my stuff: keys, smokes, coffee mug, books.

The stuff I just dropped.

"Thanks, guys." I took my items and offered them beers.

This went on night after night.

I'd get out of my truck in the dark and I'd drop things, sometimes falling in the grass.

And each time there'd be even more gnomes about eight inches tall wearing red hats.

Then it finally dawned on me.

"You sawed off bastards. If you wanna have a beer just say so."

2

Hey! Bleeker, Shindig, Moxy, Boots, Pointy, Flip, Johann, Levi, Cornwall, Lipshitz, Stony, Blumberg, Crumples,

Spot, DingDong, Trevor, Spittoon, Blade, Furio...hey, guys!

What's up, Lucky?

Hey! One of the big dipshits dropped his keys in the grass and when I found them for him he gave me a big bottle of Bud!

All bottles are big to us, Toodles.

You catch my drift.

Okay? So what? You got a beer and didn't bring us any. Ass.

Listen! The big dipshit comes home every night at the same time. I say we trip him up when he gets out of his roar machine, and then we pick his stuff up and give it to him. Then he'll give us Bud!

Heeeeeeeeey!

Right? They don't call me Lucky for nuthin'!

Safe Assumption

I could be making

an "ass" out

of "u"

and "me",

but the talking

stopped

when you

entered

the room.

All eyes were on

the lifted

bosom

the fishnet

legs

the bedroom

eyes.

Trouble with a

capital T

coming my way,

all pearly

whites

and cruel

intent.

I was never

more thankful for

my low

Testosterone.

Golden Noodles

I had a gay roommate for a semester back in college

and we got along just fine.

There are only two things I remember that I could have done without,

one visual and one verbal.

Visually.

He had a thing for Gustav Klimt and the apartment was festooned

with prints done in angles and gold.

and

Verbally.

When I asked him why he made so much pasta, he answered,

"It makes my cum taste good."

To this day I roll my eyes at the Vienna Secession Movement

and

I don't really care for spaghetti.

Red Flag

I was buck naked on the leatherette couch

while super-hot-she straddled me and gave me a right

good bang.

After the fireworks went off, she started with the

waterworks.

What's the matter? I asked.

-I'm gay.

That didn't seem gay to me.

-I'M GAY!

Maybe you're bi-sexual.

-There's no such thing!

I know a bunch of bisexuals who might disagree.

And then I reached out to try to give her a hug,

'cause that's what

you do when you've made a lesbian cry.

But she shrugged me off and gave me a glare.

-You don't OWN me. She said, slow-like to get the point across.

Yeah, I know.

-You just don't understand.

You're right, I don't.

-Wanna get high?

Absolutely. I said.

So we smoked some pretty strong stuff using a one-hitter,

except I hit it several times and I'm a light-weight to begin with.

Weed always makes me do two things - take a shit and go to sleep.

Every time. Every single time. And I'm fine with that.

So after another go at the naked Olympics on the leatherette couch

I really needed to shit.

After I clogged up the john real good and came out smelling like a rose

she told me I had to go 'cause it was getting real late.

And it was.

Okay. I said.

-Don't get mad, because you can't stay.

I'm not mad. I said Okay.

-Fine. As long as you're not mad.

Okay.

-Okay.

And I left stoned out of my fucking mind.

I was probably going about 20 mph but it felt like I was lead car in the Indianapolis 500.

The 30 minute drive took nearly two hours and once I dozed off at a
red light.

After I got home,

at long last,

and was laying splayed out on my back

I reviewed: she's gorgeous, more than two decades younger,

has very strong weed tolerance, emotionally unstable with a

sexual identity crisis.

But the only Red Flag I picked up on was she made me drive high.

Good Riddance

Decades

of dodging and weaving

staying out of reach

splitting hairs

and explaining away

Foul intentions

by any scope of

reasoning

Placating the

insecurities

of the self-crippled

Playing ignorant

to the threat

of a rabid

service animal

The days of

running interference

for the weak, the young

and the uninformed

are done

Quick and painless

if that's the way

but just go

And let us laugh

not in joy

but in relief.

Fucked Proper

An Irishman I know summed it up:

The world is fucked, man.

Turtles sunning

Necks fully stretched

catching rays

in January.

They should be two feet under

dreaming turtle dreams

dreaming of spring.

A friend posted a photo

from Indiana.

The kids had built a snowman.

A real horror.

After you build a snowman

you shouldn't see patches

of muck and grass

around the bottom of Frosty,

not in January.

As the Irishman said:

The world is fucked, man...proper.

Everything.

The kids, the turtles, the weather, the snowmen.

Properly fucked.

If It Had Been So
for MCG

If it had been so, a library of stories would have been read,

and the favorites re-read again and again.

An unknown number of questions would have been asked,

and then answered the best that I could.

If it had been so, there would have been far more laughing

and far less silence.

Hugs and smiles and knowing looks for "you had to have been there" jokes

would have been the order of the day,

in place of furrowed brows, dogged non-memories and

part-time, self-made happiness in dreams.

If it had been so, it would have been so different. If it had been so.

Advice from a Jailhouse Regular

If you find yourself doing a long stretch and

you're not into fucking guys

or getting fucked by guys,

this is what you do.

You find another inmate you can overpower,

see, and you corner that little shit.

You rip down his pants and stick the tip,

just the tip, mind you, in his ass.

This sends a clear message

that you will, indeed, fuck an ass.

It's the same principle as picking out the biggest

motherfucker in the yard and knocking him silly.

Picky

You come in here with your weirdness

and I like it.

Some of your hair is shaved

and some of it is dyed blazing red.

You have a ring in your nose

and an empty piercing hole in your lip.

Ten rings on your ten fingers,

probably some on your toes,

and a whole mess of charms and beads around your

neck.

You're slim, fit, curvy in the right places

and you're wearing a black dress with black stockings.

I look you up and down and sideways

and I like it.

However,

you might be a little long in the tooth for the look

and you may have aged out of your Goth persona,

you're hands are kinda veiny

and you speak in a monotone.

I think I'm gonna pass.

To the Death

They fought bravely,

Dying in scores by my hand,

and

I was sorely wounded.

But I dance upon the corpses of the vanquished,

Spit on their grieving widows,

and

Laugh in the faces of their crying children.

It will be a cold day in hell

Before those hornets return

and

Build another nest on my back porch.

The Man Who Works for Dogs

Walking along the beach at Kona

and sleeping beneath the palms,

you'll find a homeless man with

a small pack of equally-homeless dogs.

"How do you keep them fed?"

According to him, he has a daily route

where he stops and sweeps and hoses off

sidewalks in front of shops that cater to tourists.

"And the shop owners feed you and the dogs?"

The shop owners only feed the dogs

and he spends the rest of the day panhandling

to feed himself; the dogs look healthier than he does.

The homeless man spends at least half of the day

working, being productive, to feed his canine friends,

but doesn't work to take care of himself.

I can't decide if this is because he values himself

very highly or doesn't value himself at all.

The Price of Experience

Innocence was the price paid for experience,

good old pre-masturbation, pre-copulation,

pre-nicotine, pre-caffeine, pre-alcohol, pre-substance,

pre-politics, pre-religion, pre-judgement, pre-workforce

all-consuming innocence.

When love meant your mother,

literature meant *The Hobbit*,

entertainment meant Saturday morning cartoons and

freedom meant summer vacation.

Everything that followed killed innocence,

everything that followed - was experience,

and it slit the throat of innocence

and drank its blood.

Hip Shot

Folks don't like it

when you shoot from the hip

because that lines you up with their genitalia,

or in close proximity.

And nobody likes taking a shot to the baby-makers,

or in close proximity.

Remember that the next time you fire off a

verbal nut shot,

    sack wack,

    ball rack

    jewel flicker,

    or hog wrangler.

And let's not forget the ladies.

They don't appreciate a

verbal egg cracker,

    cherry popper,

vag smacker,

lip splitter

or twat twister.

If you gotta shoot from the hip,

angle up and

get 'em right between the eyes.

It's only polite.

J.D. & Me
for Jessup Digby

I met J. D. in a very roundabout way.

Over the course of months, maybe years,

I saw him many times before we actually spoke.

He seemed to live at the edge of my periphery,

in the next line, a few people further back

or sitting at the light of oncoming traffic,

maybe coming in the in door while I was

going out the out door.

Until one day, I was feeling very low,

he stood right in front of me,

squinting and grinning.

The light wasn't so bright, so I asked,

"What are you squinting at?"

"You," he said, "I'm squinting at you."

That was pretty weird and I didn't know what

to say to it, and he continued,

"You're trying to figure out what to say to that, aren't you?"

I just looked at him.

"Just say it, man. Say what you wanna say?"

"Okay, I answered. "Knock off the squinting, I'm not here for you to squint at. What's your goddamned problem?

He smiled big at this and stuck out his hand for a shake, and I took it.

He pumped my hand a few times and said,

"There you go, man. We're gonna get along just fine."

G.R.G. & I

I watched G- for a good long while,

dumb bastard,

always trying to do the right thing

the wrong way.

Always getting his tit in a wringer,

crossing against traffic,

striking out with the bases loaded.

People walked all over him,

figured him for a soft touch,

an easy mark,

I watched it time and again

and he wasn't catching on.

The users weren't wrong,

G-'s worn out sense of

integrity and scruples were

a liability in this day and age

leaving him drained in every possible way,

from his bank of emotions to his

bank account,

and everything in between.

He assumed the best of people,

usually experienced the worst.

I finally got my fill of watching

this sad sack flounder,

so I popped in and made my acquaintance.

The old boy's been on the

right track ever

since.

fool no longer

the next time I go

will be be the

last time

I go.

I have gone many

times before

but always

returned.

for there were reasons

emotional ties and

connections

before.

those are all but gone

now into dust and

only one still

remains.

as mater meets her maker

a fool no longer

as chains are

broken.

Holidays
for MCG

Christmases aren't merry.

Thanksgivings aren't happy.

New Years aren't even new,

they're just years.

No hearts on Valentine's Days.

No scares on Halloweens.

Fireworks don't pop on July 4ths,

they're damp with tears.

Holidays are only Days

because you're not here.

Mantis Boy

The male mantis goes in knowing that

once be busts his nut he's got only

a matter of seconds, or less, to

get the fuck out of there.

Yet he goes for it, indeed.

He'll find a lady mantis,

however that's achieved,

and dance around

until the lady mantis lets him in close,

then BAM he's on her,

banging away mantis style

until SPLOOSH!

gets it done.

This is no time to reflect on how awesome

that lady mantis pussy was,

no time to roll over and have a smoke,

get your senses together

and your legs back under you.

Flee, Mantis Boy, Flee!

Nope.

She ate his head right off.

That's how pissed a lady mantis

gets if she doesn't come.

Sound familiar?

Fine Young Cannibal

Another dull shift at the register

and I was leaning against the counter

to take some weight off my feet.

In walked a local representative of

law and order, a polite, handsome, young guy,

a regular with a badge.

– How're you tonight?

I'm good. Yourself?

– Not so bad.

Actually, I'm starving. You guys got any sandwiches left?

– There are some left on the rack, have a peek.

The cop went over to the sandwich rack, took a look,

and came walking back with a sandwich wrapped

in shiny silver foil.

– What did you find?

Pulled pork.

I wrinkled up my nose in disgust and shook my head.

– Ugh!

What?

– Cannibal.

He stopped walking towards the register, tilted his head to the side and closed his eyes, a half-grin sneaking out.

He looked at me with his hands resting on his gun belt.

Really?

– Just to let you know, officer, we're on camera right now.

Advice to Young Girls

My dear young ladies,

listen well.

Get it through your

pretty, thick skulls

and don't make

the same blunders

your mothers made.

A rock hard cock

is not love.

It isn't there to

hurt you,

no ma'am, but

each and every one

of them is on

a lust-fueled mission

to pleasurably conquer

and lay low

dreams and aspirations

of unwary wombs.

That's the very

nature of their

design.

The Day Phleebit Came to Town

Sitting in my truck on the edge of a field

smoking a Lucky and drinking pink lemonade,

minding my own business, what there is of it,

while thinking about suicide for the millionth time.

It was a muggy, dark night with clouds in the sky

and so I didn't notice the V4 Oort Cruiser

parked in the middle of a couple of dozen cows,

chewing their cuds and also minding their own

business.

When out of the dark a figure approached me.

Phleebit was about seven feet tall and thin as a rake,

except for his bulbous head, and he had three eyes,

no nose to speak of and a big smiling pie hole.

"Hey, there, Earthling. I'm Phleebit.

I'm in 3rd Recon and Exploratory

for the Galactic Mini Mall Conglomerate.

That's my V4 Oort Cruiser parked over yonder amongst the bovine. I sure do like your Ford. Is that a '95?"

I took the .45 from my lap and shot that alien right where his nose should have been.

Yeah, the plan was to blow my own brains out, but no way was I gonna let that smooth talking piece of shit give us

another mini mall.

Being Human is Tragic Enough Without the Window Dressing.

Hi..

Nice to mee...

Yes, I'm...

Uh...

Okay, yeah...

STOP!

You feel that you are pansexual with polyamorous tendencies and you're pretty sure you're comfortable with he/him pronouns which works out because you were born biologically male, what with the penis and five o'clock shadow and all, and assigned said gender by the white colonial patriarchy, which you know well being white yourself, and you are dealing with childhood traumas caused by a lack of fatherly mentorship at an early age and thus are medicated to cope with triggers from strangers who are unaware of the past aggressions both macro and micro that you have suffered and you work in a pit bull rescue and can't believe that so many people would be so callous as to abandon entire litters of pups right out in front of the dog pound and you are trying to be a vegan but you're having trouble finding a suitable protein substitute that doesn't cause more trouble with your lactose intolerance and you feel really guilty about that because it clashes with your spiritual journey but you keep forgetting to ask your primary health care provider about it because your ADHD and OCD and nervousness caused by vape withdrawal leave you scatterbrained, so much so that you were unable to attend the rallies to have Thomas Jefferson removed from the history books, thus causing you to miss out on revenue that you would have earned by selling beaded necklaces to the protestors, and you worked really hard on that jewelry, but you were counting on that money to help you get to Burning Man with your friends and now they're going to trip on psilocybin in the desert without you.

Very interesting.

By the way,

what's your name?

Rarities

To inconvenience one's self

for another

is actually very common.

To do so without complaint,

however,

is as rare as true love.

Beautiful Death

She shines with an inner light;

Pulsing pink and lime neon,

And like moths to flame

They die brittle on the edge

Of lust-induced splendor.

Burning Innovators

The clock brought order out of chaos.

Put time to work for us

And us to work for time.

Now we know where to be

Every minute of every hour

Of every day of every week

Of every month of every year

Until we live our final

Tick Tock.

The second hand is a whip

On the back

The hour hand is a splinter

Under the nail

And only dying will make

Time irrelevant once again.

The men who invented

Mechanical time-keeping

Wrung the life from life

And are surely burning in the

Bowels of Hell.

Requiem for a Varmint

I tried.

I really did.

But you shot

right out there

furious furry flurry.

I had hope

for a second

but then felt

the rear tire

go over a

bump

where there

are no

bumps.

You can see

in the dark.

You wash your food

before you eat.

You unlatch latches

and turn door knobs

and use the pet door.

But you haven't evolved

to the point

to dodge

loud bright monsters

traveling in straight lines.

Tonight, sadly,

I removed one

from your

gene pool.

Rest In Peace,

Dumb-ass raccoon.

All Is Well At Rock Bottom

Rock Bottom gets a bad rap

It's a great place to be if you let it take you

At Rock Bottom you don't have to worry about jack shit

Things aren't going to get any worse

"Well, you can still die" they say

But at Rock Bottom death is a step up so bring it on

At Rock Bottom you can drop the baggage and the

pretense

Hope and Love and Disappointment and Aspiration,

Good and Bad and Loss become beasts of legend

Probably never real to begin with

At Rock Bottom you eat and drink,

sleep and shit,

work if you can,

screw if you can,

breathe and blink

If you can do half of these things each day it's a check in the win column

But nobody is keeping score anyway

At Rock Bottom you don't have to keep up the act

You can sweat indifference,

piss disregard and spit truth

Others push their silly

mythologies realities formalities moralities on you

Grin and joke it away

No call for that crap at Rock Bottom.

Stay in Bed

There are so few really good reasons to get out of bed

most days.

At least, that's what I've found in my case.

I know people roll out in the morning, freshly showered

or not,

to put in the hours for someone,

in order to draw a paycheck for someone else.

Men bust their asses doing dangerous shit, or worse,

boring shit,

while a dude in unstained clothes with unstained hands

barks and belittles.

Then they're paid, and after the bills are taken care of

and

the baby birds at home are fed and equipped,

and the breeding mare gets her nails and hair done,

what's left for them?

Eddie Murphy answered that question best back in the '80s;

he gets the big piece of chicken.

What a fucking rip-off.

That's the reward for falling in love, getting married,

dealing with children,

starting a family phone plan,

vacationing in Branson (again),

destroying the body, mind and soul.

I don't know how they do it.

Even more, how they continue doing it.

How they fall into believing their life is preferable to

putting

a shotgun in their mouth and blowing their

dead hopes and dreams

against the wood paneling of their man cave.

That splatter, a little on the neon beer sign, a dab on the

baseball jersey,

maybe a chunk of gray matter atop their gaming

system,

would be the most original of their creations.

The wives have it no better.

Many of them choose to stay home to

"take care of the house and kids".

Their men come home disgruntled and bitter, looking

for their

big piece of chicken,

what happened to that handsome, sweet guy that used

to take me parking down by the river?

He's long dead, honey baby.

Their own hopes and dreams are sloughed out into a

pan

along with the afterbirth

following the arrival of each of their baby birds, lookalike parasites hanging from their tits and purses for close to two decades, or longer.

What a horrible waste of potential is the traditional nuclear family.

Don't get out of bed.

Don't fall in love. Just fall in lust.

Love is just tired lust in disguise anyway.

Just stop at the fucking.

Fuck, fuck and fuck some more, everyone is happy.

But get the old snip snip, guys, get the tubes tied, gals.

Don't ruin it by duplicating yourselves; you're not that great.

Stick to your own abode, shun cohabitation.

Oil and water don't mix.

Do your own thing and on your own terms.

Work for yourself, do for yourself, make something for yourself.

Of course, doing things my way could mean the end of the human race.

But would that be such a bad thing?

Fist Fight

Who do you think would win

in a fist fight,

a young Mark Twain or

a young Ernest Hemingway?

Ernie was known for being

a bad-ass man's man,

but Sam was wily and verbose.

I can envision Ernie getting

sloppy following some piercing

verbal zingers,

giving Sam the chance to

sweep in on humorists' feet,

dancing and zig-zagging

as he landed jab after jab.

A different story, though,

if Ernie actually got hands on Sam.

Ernie would grapple him into

a pretzel.

I don't know…

But one thing is for sure.

Sam and Ernie could both take

John Steinbeck.

Johnny's ass would be grass.

I can hear Sam now,

"I'll show your grapes some wrath, fella!"

And Ernie would be standing there

with his shotgun

just in case.

Big Gals and Skinny Dudes

Surely you've noticed,

as I have,

there are a great many couplings

between

big gals and skinny dudes.

I say "big" not to sound mean;

when I say "big" I mean "fat",

just to be clear.

I wonder why that is?

Is it because of the physics involved?

I mean,

two fatties would have

a real tough time

fuckin',

unless the fat guy has a

monster hog,

am I right?

But a skinny dude could have

an average

run-of-the-mill dick

and still manage to

get up in there,

and get the deed done.

Do you think

they are

naturally drawn

to one another?

That somehow

biology

is telling the big gal

"hey, get that

skinny dude.

He'll get the job

done."

Nature is mysterious

and I'm just glad the

big gals

and the

skinny dudes

have someone.

Casualty

You say you're

thirty

and you've dodged the marriage bullet

a few times.

That may be true,

but you have

four kids by

four different men.

You may have dodged the marriage bullets

but you've been poked

full of holes by

bayonets.

A Royal Death

Sitting in the back seat, going down the highway.

Mom behind the wheel,

her little sister riding shotgun.

They sang and bebopped along to the radio,

dancing in their seats.

It was a bright, hot, sunny, summer day;

August 17th 1977 to be exact.

The song on the radio stopped mid-lyric for a

breaking news report.

The voice spoke in grave tones,

saying words that prompted

mom to pull over to the side of the road

blinded by tears.

I could see a hundred cars on the highway,

none of them in motion.

Mom and her sister sat crying and holding hands,

and I heard the radio say again:

"The King is Dead".

Kick a Man When He's Down

The Jews

were forced to wear

yellow Stars of David.

They were also

forced to buy the stars

they were

forced to wear.

Imagine having to

fork out the funds

to target

yourself for

Extermination.

There were even

instances in which

Jews were murdered

and the families

of the dead were

hit up for the

cost of the

Bullets.

The Nazis

really were

Masters of

adding

Insult to Injury.

Any Given Night in Seoul ROK

"Hey, Jude" blares from the doors of countless

noraebang,

out of tune and most of the words mispronounced.

You have to watch your step and navigate around

puddles of orange vomit,

a mix of *soju* and *kimchi*, in too-large amounts,

created those.

Greasy pimps, and their crews, pass out flyers or just

scatter them on the ground,

though officially this industry doesn't exist.

Young women in too-short dresses scream in pitches

only dogs can hear

while their young men apologize profusely and offer

them trinkets.

The bars have cool, eclectic names done up in expensive

neon,

but inside they all look the same, not bad, just the same.

On every corner is an *ajumma* selling *gimbap* or *dakkochi* or *tteokbokki*,

and it's delicious, and it probably won't give you food poisoning, maybe.

Packs of office workers, still in neckties, hold hands and stumble as one,

this is the most free and uninhibited they'll ever feel.

Food delivery guys on scooters zoom by in the streets and on sidewalks,

every now and then their big metal food boxes take out a pedestrian's knee.

Older men, managers and supervisors and CEOs,

in shiny suits stand tall,

their underlings flicking lighters for the honor of lighting their cigarettes.

Rats scurry along the curbs, and the homeless and insane scurry with them,

but nobody seems to notice any of them.

Seoul is a dynamic place and a lot of fun when you're young,

but it'll make you old real quick.

soju: a clear distilled alcoholic beverage

kimchi: fermented cabbage/vegetables

noraebang: singing room/karaoke bar

ajumma: middle-aged woman

gimbap: rice, vegetables, fish or meat rolled in dried seaweed and sliced bite size

dakkochi: grilled chicken on a stick

tteokbokki: spicy rice cakes

The Authority

You try to have a conversation,

just some face-to-face interaction,

because maybe you're killing time between tasks

or genuinely craving some legitimate connection.

Forgive the rhyming, it was purely coincidental

and if it happens again it'll be mostly incidental.

Couldn't resist. *Mea culpa.*

Anyway, so you start talking to the guy

and right off the bat you hear he's very nasal,

and that throws you off, but you persist in the spirit

of not being hastily judgemental.

But in addition to the fact that he talks through his nose,

he does so at a volume that comes across as dominant,

authoritative and a little aggressive.

Again, though, you're not trying to judge, so you keep

it going, maybe you can glean something worth hearing out of his jet engine pronouncements.

So you run the gauntlet, from classic literature to modern cinema,

from the problems with women to the best attributes of women,

from how we can do better as men to what is perfectly fine about us,

from the weather in Bali to the political climate in Luxembourg.

You get the picture.

Problem is, the guy already has his mind made up and you're nothing but a prop for him to bounce his voice off of.

He's an Authority. On which topic? Well, fucking all of them, of course.

Charles Dickens is overrated and Tarantino should have stopped at six films.

Women want equal rights but not equal responsibility but they are soft and smell nice.

Men could be less aggressive towards each other but our beards are really cool.

Bali is getting hotter with water levels rising and nothing new is happening in Luxembourg.

Every sentence he yells has a big, fat period at the end, no discussion, topic terminated.

So where do you go from there?

There's nowhere to go from there.

Whatever you throw out there he's going to sink it and drown it

in a puddle of obnoxious, biased wheeze-words at full blast.

But I tried and that's what counts.

The Giant

I was sitting on the porch and watching the squirrels

dart from tree to tree

when I heard a rustling coming from a pile of dead

leaves.

The rustling from the leaves grew closer and

out of the pile

walked a little man

wearing a hat made from a mouse head and carrying a

walking stick.

He saw me staring and yelled, "What are you looking

at?"

"What are you?" I asked.

The little man rolled his eyes and strutted over to the

porch.

"I'm a giant, you dumb asshole," he said and pointed his stick at me.

"But you're so small," I said.

"Not where I come from, man," then he cocked his mouse head and walked away.

600

2,609 weeks

18,263 days

438,312 hours

26,298,720 minutes

1,577,923,200 seconds

600 months ago on a Sunday

the middle of the afternoon

very convenient

after church

but before dinner.

nobody asked for permission

none was certainly given

the swimmer went the distance

and cracked that egg

wide open.

do this, do that

don't do this, don't do that

learn this, but forget about that

strive for this, avoid that at all costs

nobody spouts the same spiel.

the imaginary friend was refused

almost immediately

fairness, honesty and goodness

was kept intact - mostly -

for any other way to be made no sense.

go to school

a bag of pencils, a ruler, some paste

and a shit ton of books

cram it in your head

keep what you need and move on.

don't be like me

don't do what I did

do what you wanna do

but make it good, man

you only have the one shot.

go there, look at that

try these, do more of the same

steer straight and don't swerve

keep the promises

but don't expect like in return.

600 months will keep you busy

so much to do

there is no way to do it all

and after a while

you realize it's going to be incomplete.

So fast and so slow

more of the relativity

a gift from Albert

I'm sure we knew it anyway

even without the nifty name.

maybe in another

600 months

it'll be time to pack it in

maybe on a Sunday afternoon.

50 is a nice round number.

Eggs and Toast

It had been a good night.

What we could remember of it.

My buddy, Scott, and me had

painted Phuket red. Two coats.

We sat outside our cheap beach hotel

looking at our toast and eggs.

Pushing eggs around with forks,

attempting to piece the night together.

As Scott recalled a Malaysian hooker,

a big brown rat sprung from the bushes.

The rat stood on its hind legs on the dining patio,

twitching, looking left and right, tense and frantic.

It was huge, the size of a medium-sized cat,

we dropped our forks and watched it.

"That's a big fucking rat," Scott said.

Then the rat raced away into the bushes again.

We went back to our eggs and toast and

talked about the Malaysian hooker, briefly.

For out of the same bushes from where the rat arrived

plodded a big monitor lizard, four feet long easily.

The lizard's tongue was flicking at the patio, smelling,

obviously sniffing out the trail of the rat.

"That's a big fucking lizard," Scott said.

The lizard found the scent and darted back into the bushes.

We went back to our food, pushing it around, Scott remembered the Malaysian hooker's name.

Yellow Fever

I was in a bar

drinking, of course,

and hitting on girls,

of course.

To be specific, I was

in a bar in South Korea

and I was hitting on

Korean girls.

Another guy at the bar,

a Korean guy,

took exception to

my wooing of the ladies

and loudly slurred

through soju-scented breath

that I was afflicted with

Yellow Fever.

"Dumbshit," I said,

"as the only girls here are Korean,

that's who I'm talking to.

If I was in a Kenyan bar,

would I have Black Fever?

Brown Fever if I was

in Bogota?

White Fever in Moscow?"

He thought about it

for a second and then

shook his head

in understanding.

More booze was

bought and I now

had a wing man.

His help with the

language barrier went

a long way in

getting me laid.

Loins

A common theme I came across in my readings of

The Iliad and The Odyssey by the Greek Homer,

in the ancient epics of Gilgamesh and Beowulf,

in The Torah of the Hebrews and The Labors of Hercules,

was the girding of loins,

not a completely familiar undertaking personally

experienced.

But in honor of these ancient warriors of poetry,

scripture, historical accounts and mythological

allegories,

I girded my loins in a show of masculine solidarity.

However, in the process of girding up,

I wound up wearing a pair of lacy ladies' underwear

and developed a hernia, so I'm not all that sure I got it

right.

One should always leave the girding of loins to the professionals.

Chemical Warfare

The Dragon sits alert

in the depths of the

cerebrum.

Always on watch

Looking for, and expecting,

trouble.

It feels tingles in its

lustrous scales;

warning.

The Goblins are on

the move

again.

They move swiftly towards

the long-toothed

sentry.

Swinging gibbon-like

hand-over-hand down

synapses.

A fight is coming

in a screeching

horde.

The Goblins want

the Dragon

dead.

Only then will

their terror

reign.

The Dragon only

flexes its battle-worn talons;

grinning.

Trade In
For MCG

I've stood in awe at the silence within Notre Dame, climbed the steps of the Eiffel Tower

and people watched for hours on end from cafes on

Parisian corners.

I've stumbled drunkenly across the Charles Bridge and

watched the clock chime,

while searching for the Green Man's face at the Stare

Mesto.

I've cruised Sydney Harbor, hiked in a turpentine tree

forest near the Three Sisters

and bought a didgeridoo from an Aborigine fellow.

I've had ice in my hair

and watched killer whales off the coast of Victoria.

I stood with six million strangers in Times Square in

single-digit temps

to watch a bright ball drop to signal the start of 1997,

and was then kissed and groped by a short, chubby Australian.

I've knelt before golden Buddha's with ruby eyes and listened to the mellow gong of the bell calling monks to prayer.

I've contemplated the chilled waters of Lake Louise with only a porcupine for company.

I've parasailed through a Bahamian sky tied to the back of a speedboat driven by a man holding a bottle of rum.

I've been in a bar fight with Russians just because the vodka was flowing and it seemed like the thing to do.

I've walked the humid streets of Hong Kong after a meal of duck feet and jellyfish.

I've peered through the fog of Milford Sound and slept under the stars of Aotearoa me Te Waipounamu.

I've stood on the top of skyscrapers that have since been destroyed by fanatics and madmen.

I've written my name in the snow on Jungfrau and read the words of Mark Twain left at Lucerne.

I've dived in the Korean Straits in 30-degree water just to see white starfish and to watch sea slugs mate on the side of an underwater mountain.

I've been packed like a sardine in a subway car at rush hour and slurped up udon noodles in Tokyo.

I've flown over a volcano in a helicopter, teared up at Pearl Harbor, watched sea turtles and manta rays from my hotel balcony, and ate roast pig and poi at a luau.

The things I've seen and marveled at with these eyes,

the Grand Canyon, the Rocky Mountains, the Alps,

the Pacific and Atlantic Oceans, the South China and North China,

the Sea of Japan, the Mediterranean, the Channel,

the castle at Heidelberg, the Louvre, giant magnolia trees in Singapore,

polar ice caps from 40,000 feet, the Mekong in Vietnam,

Green Day, Eric Clapton, Billy Joel, AC/DC, too many concerts, musicals and performances to name,

performers putting on naughty shows in Bangkok,

French street walkers, hookers in windows,

keas, kangaroos, sharks swimming under me, angry monkeys in trees,

alligators from bridges at water level, geckos on my TV screen,

Omaha Beach, Mannequin Pis, the canals of Amsterdam, the gondolas of Venice, the Colosseum and the Spanish Steps, Key West at sunset and Hemingway's House,

the prairies of the Dakotas, the streets of Toronto, a fleabag motel in Albuquerque,

the Space Needle, Alaskan fjords, otters fighting over a fish in the Buffalo River...

It goes on and on.

And on.

But I'll tell you what.

I'd trade it all in a heartbeat

just to

hear

your

heart

beat.

Lowest of the Low

Habitual liars, warmongers and whoremongers.

Greedy fat cats, con-men and corporate men.

They are pretty low.

Spouse and child abusers, puppy kickers.

Rip off artists that leave the elderly destitute.

They are really low.

Bullies and cheaters and belittlers,

busybodies, gossips and charlatans.

So damned low.

But the lowest of the low.

The very lowest of the low.

The bottom rung of the low ladder,

roommates with Satan low,

line 'em up against the wall with no last cigarette low,

are the ones who take the last piece of pizza

but didn't help pay for it.

Goofy Food Shit

I've heard some goofy shit in my life.

I have a nephew who dislikes "wet" food and won't eat soup or stew or gumbo.

How do you explain the cereal I know you eat?

Hypocrite.

Other people won't eat bananas or sushi because they don't like the texture.

These are people that have never gone hungry a day in their lives.

Every food has a texture until you chew it; then it all has the same texture.

Mushy.

And there are other people who won't eat if the different foods touch each other on the plate.

Goes in and out the same holes, people. Seriously.

The tastes compliment each other, it's a whole "thing".

Separatist.

I knew a guy who wouldn't eat pecans, but not because he didn't like how they tasted.

He couldn't decide if it's pronounced "puh-cahns" or "pee-cans" and he wouldn't take sides.

That seems like a mental illness of some sort to me; at least a minor condition.

Nutjob.

My own dear mother has a problem eating meat if it looks like part of an animal.

It has to be cut and sliced and fileted and diced and deboned until it's unidentifiable.

I understand being an animal lover, but carnivores need the protein.

Bleeding heart.

I suppose I'm just as guilty with the goofy food shit, if I'm being honest.

I prefer watermelon with seeds because the seedless just looks wrong.

I refrain from eating bacon because it's too popular.

I eat bread heels, but only in pairs in a sandwich because it feels like a reunion.

I like grapes, but nothing "grape flavored".

Just eat it and live for fuck's sake.

The Stardust High Horse

I am Stardust.

I was born from

the Cosmos,

infinitely linked

to the

Heavens!

A Catalyst of

Transformation,

From Stardust

to Life

to ME!

The same goes

for the

chicken

I had for dinner

last night.

She was born of

Stardust, too.

Linked to the

Cosmos...Life...

Heavens...Catalyst...

Transformation...

yada yada yada

See where that

got her.

Speaking of the Dead

The most interesting details

about people

are not often mentioned in

their eulogies.

My uncle snuggled with kittens,

he'd put them under his chin and

hold them, smiling

when nobody watched.

My grandma laughed deceptively;

she laughed quietly when

she was really tickled,

and loudly at slight amusements.

My grandpa was a macho man

but he was aware of the limitations in

others and didn't put them down

for coming up short.

My dad wasn't as tough as he acted;

I never told him, but I saw him cry

a couple of times when he was alone;

I can only wonder why.

And you can bet the most relevant

and telling details about you

will never get mentioned

when your turn in

the box comes

around.

A Lesson Hardly Learned

Had a fire in the kitchen

making toast.

I have a two slice toaster

but it identifies as a

four-slicer.

I told the toaster

it's dangerous to

stuff four slices

in two slots.

But it wouldn't

listen and now

I just

eat

cold

bread.

Gary R. Gowers is currently a resident with the Osage Artists Community (OAC) in Belle, Missouri. He spends his time writing prose, poetry and screenplays, taking photographs and ingesting far too many books, podcasts and movies. He also enjoys sitting on his porch, smoking Luckies, drinking coffee and yelling at squirrels.

www.ingramcontent.com/pod-product-compliance
Lightning Source LLC
Chambersburg PA
CBHW051824090426
42736CB00011B/1630